IN THE
PRESENCE
OF
MOTHERS

Books by Judith Minty

Lake Songs and Other Fears   1974
Yellow Dog Journal   1979
Letters to My Daughters   1980

IN THE
PRESENCE
OF MOTHERS

Judith Minty

UNIVERSITY OF PITTSBURGH PRESS

With thanks to William Heyen, Roderick Jellema, Joseph Keller, and Robert VanderMolen, who read portions of this manuscript in its early stages.

Published by the University of Pittsburgh Press, Pittsburgh, Pa. 15260
Copyright © 1981, Judith Minty
All rights reserved
Feffer and Simons, Inc., London
Manufactured in the United States of America

Library of Congress Cataloging in Publication Data

Minty, Judith
In the presence of mothers.

(Pitt poetry series)
I. Title.
PS3563.I48I5   811'.54   80-5259
ISBN 0-8229-3427-2
ISBN 0-8229-5321-8 (pbk.)

*The publication of this book is supported by grants
from the National Endowment for the Arts
in Washington, D.C., a Federal agency,
and the Pennsylvania Council on the Arts.*

Acknowledgment is made to the following publications, which first published some of the poems in this book: *The GVSC Review, Heartland II, The Missouri Review, Mundus Artium, Original Sin, The Sound of a Few Leaves, Southern Poetry Review, Sou'wester, Sycamore, waves,* and *The Yellow Magazine.*

"The End of Summer" appears in *50 Contemporary Poets: The Creative Process,* edited by Alberta T. Turner, © 1977 by Longman Inc. "Look to the Back of the Hand," first appeared in an issue of *Poetry* and was reprinted in *The Poetry Anthology, 1912-1977,* Daryl Hine and Joseph Parisi, editors, Houghton Mifflin Company, Boston, 1978. "Palmistry for Blind Mariners," "Prowling the Ridge," and "Harbors" appear in *The Third Coast, Contemporary Michigan Poetry,* Conrad Hilberry, Herbert Scott, and James Tipton, editors, Wayne State University Press, Detroit, 1976.

"Last Rights" first appeared in *The Barat Review,* 7, no. 2, copyright 1979 by Barat College. "Raven" is reprinted from *The Carleton Miscellany,* copyrighted by Carleton College, August 29, 1978. "The House That Is Deserted by Mothers" was originally published in a special issue of *Connections.* "Before Completion" and "Winter Poem/Snowy Owl" first appeared in *The Great Lakes Review.* "Finding a Depth," © 1978, The New Yorker Magazine, Inc. "Grand Valley," "Harbors," "Look to the Back of the Hand," "Palmistry for Blind Mariners," and "Sailing by Stars" originally appeared in the March 1974 issue of *Poetry,* and are reprinted by permission. "Yellow Dog" was originally published in *Poetry Northwest,* XVI, no. 1 (Spring 1975), and was copyrighted by the University of Washington. "The Lake Road" and "The Back Roads" were first published in *Red Cedar Review.*

The line by Robert Duncan appears in his book, *Bending the Bow,* copyright © 1968 by Robert Duncan, and is reprinted by permission of New Directions. The quote from Anais Nin is from *The Diary of Anais Nin, 1931-1934,* Harcourt Brace Jovanovich, Inc., New York, 1977.

For my mother,

for our Mother

CONTENTS

# At Sea

Those grand fresh-water seas of ours,—Erie, and Ontario, and Huron, and Superior, and Michigan, . . . they know what shipwrecks are, for out of sight of land, they have drowned full many a midnight ship with all its shrieking crew.

—Herman Melville

PALMISTRY FOR BLIND MARINERS

1. The Dunes

The hand: an island surrounded by oceans,
five sisters joined in a circle.
Past this desert of shifting sand, green
gropes for roots in the cup of the palm.
Forget the thumb. It's on the other side
and we dare not chart that course yet
through those reefs of birth and death.

Even here, close to shore, we're in danger.
This lake curls its tongue
round the point and the land strikes
back. Tree stumps spear at our hull
and wolves howl gale warnings.
When the wind shifts, let out the chute.
Run with it, head North for open water.

2. Heart Line

This channel is long, sounds fathoms
deep, a river that runs
through Muskegon, Grand Rapids, Lansing,
forks off toward Detroit.
But those narrows are death and we cannot
cruise them for, oh sailors,
there are so many here to love.
Stay. Drop anchor. Drift back with the current.

Let the stream wash
over years as it slices your wrist.
Feel the chill of empty rooms change
as hands burn your body and blankets
cocoon around skin
that beads with the fear of new knowledge.
Cry out the old pain,
the breaking, the separating, move on
as whispers tremble to banks.

Touch willow branches with fingertips.
Swim after trout.
Listen for laughter. It is there in the night
fires, the call of cats, in the eagle's wing
when he hunkers down from the sun.
Weave water lilies into garlands and give them
as gifts. Gather stones for your house.
Live here always, if you can.

3. The North Woods

Summer passes too quickly.
Winter brings pain. The past
dries like strawflowers.
We must change camp before withering
begins. In this Indian summer
the sun lowers its flame
over the lake, ignites
on flint stone of the Chippewa fathers.

Our canoe is ready, stripped bark
from birch trees. We will travel light,
eat berries and roots
along the way, leave footprints in sand.
Deer will drink from our hands
and the hoot of owls will guide us.
But I warn you, there will be
wailing and a beating of breasts.

Dip your paddle as you pass the bear,
asleep at the foot of her dune,
who mourns cubs, lost
in the crossing from Wisconsin.
Forget love rites and matings
and children. Bury them
deep under Mercury's mound.
This lake and mothers are cruel.

Hold close to the calm
of fingers, pass gulls who curse
from their rookery.
Let fog cling like webs
to your face, your hair. Glide
into whispers of vapor.
Grope for land if you wish. Go ashore
if you are tired of seafaring.

For my part, I know this hand
and cannot turn in again.
If you must, follow me. I am going
past the islands out
into the lake. There is a place
I have heard of where you can sink
deep into the center of dreams, where waves
will rock you in sleep, where everything
is as you wished it to be.

BEGINNINGS

Oh my mother, I always meant
to sleep close to your breasts,
in that valley of the old sea.
How could I memorize then
the motion. It comes in slow waves
after minute nicks
to the skin, after the sun
has etched us, and we curl back
to the child again. Now
in this greening light, I cast off
my lines, allow the slide,
the slow passage over water.

FINDING A DEPTH

North Channel/Lake Huron

I

These North Channel islands are forgotten children
of the glacier. Some sink
in beards of grass.
Others, like oases, sprout umbrella trees out of rock.
Clusters, buds in the center of water.
So many, so alike that each, heavily wooded,
each, stony beached, becomes the other.

At a family reunion when I was a child,
I remember being spun,
groping to find cousins and brother
in the dark behind my blindfold,
crying when I stood alone in the field.

II

The beach is so rocky I must
wear shoes for protection. Stones
clatter and crawl under my feet. White and flat,
they blend like a big Irish family.

I bend, pick one up, and flicking my wrist
send it out over the lake.
Another and another.
I am not very adept at this game. Still
one comes alive and with five
great, slanting skips goes far before sinking.

III

In this cove, with only this boat
anchored in the sunlight, I sit facing reeds.
The Channel beach at my back is piled
with flat, white stones.

I have been watching a beaver glide in and out
of shadow. It occurs to me
that a person, if she wanted, could disappear here,
name and position lost
like a misplaced photo from an album,
the loss felt here, in the chest,
a flat sinking into self.

SAILING BY STARS

We chart from stars, lay to among islands,
night like thick hair around us and
cold water knocking at the keel.
Up on deck we lean back
in a skin of mist to look for Orion's belt.

When you reach to touch me, the earth
tips, our boat sails through islands of stars.
I sink with a bear's black fur.
You drift in a dog's coat. We leave
a trail of fire searing across the sky.

LOOK TO THE BACK OF THE HAND

It is a water hand, this right one,
changed by the will and actions;
fingers long and tapering, palm
not thick or calloused, skin
clear, yet slightly flushed with emotion:
the hand perhaps of an artist.
Do not look at the back of this hand.

The finger of Apollo reaches long
into creativity: seeker who never finds self.
The thumb rises strong, supple
with generosity, stretching toward ambition.
Benevolence, platonic love,
devotion are read in the mounts.
Do not turn this hand over.

It is an atlas surrounded by lakes,
full of paths and roads, hills valleys plains.
Lines intersect, fork off,
chain—yet the signs remain.
It erodes with years, wears
my signature, and I cannot change it.
"Hair on the back of the hand
denotes extreme cruelty in a woman."

PREPARATIONS FOR ENDINGS

Even in the fire of touching
a stone, in the falling
of new rivers,
in the light of paths that pulled
out of woods, I knew I would turn
into the hollow of myself
and sail back to lakes.

A pinecone, two leaves,
words that flew about
on a crumpled piece of paper,
all stored in deep pockets
for my fingers to turn
as the stranger's voice rose
like bright birds off the mountain.

When I lived in your dark
forest, I almost lost
the other place. "It is close
to shore. You can tumble in waves.
The sun roars there
and once I caught the wind
and soared over water."

Leaves wither, my boat
bleats in the harbor.
We face each other. My hands
flutter up with broken wings,
but you turn, and they fall.
What more, what more was there
to say in that narrow passage?

DESCENTS

Once she was brave.
Arms gripped to chest,
she turned her back on the pines,
stepped down through ice
into waves. With great "ahs"
she pushed out
from the land's arm,
faced the falling eye of the sun.

Feet and hands
curl hard into fists,
shadows of fins. Now she
glides beneath the surface.
Gills expanding, contracting, she shivers
with the current, lengthens
her belly against the lake's floor
and murmurs to others like her.
They speak of glory in this wetness,
this stroking of scales.

When trunks twist and sigh
in the swamp, they sink deeper.
When branches creak,
when roots scratch in the mud,
they roll to the light and listen.
Shuddering back and forth
they walk on tails, swim with hands,
misfits torn between water and land.

HARBORS

Sailboats anchored in the cove
turn with the wind at evening
as if they hear music.
They bow to shore. And the sun,
torn by gray clouds,
sinks into the wild island.

In August we turn to a harbor
where forests of masts
stand planted in wells. The boats
bob and clank their tambourine halyards
as if they wanted to dance again,
their spars cutting the moon.

On that island the dead forest
rises from sleep. When winds howl
and the moon turns round,
an echo begins.
Gray masts glide from the swamp,
leap and spin over the empty bay,
hair whirling behind them.

GALE WARNING

In this deepest hole of the night,
so dark I can't tell
if my eyes are open or shut,
I huddle at the tiller and try to conjure my people
around me. The lake heaves and falls,
it spins me around, reaches out to pull me down.

Those stones from shore, the old square-jawed ones
and children, I need
their eyes for light on the deck,
their lips calling my name.
For this mast shudders with change, a shifting
of winds. It bends hard against the sea.

When a moon breaks the sky,
when this north wind dies, I will
lift up out of bad dreams, wait for night
to run its course, for port off the bow.
I know the signal, it's "red right returning,"
and I'm trying. Oh all of you, I am coming home.

WITNESS

On September 26, 1930, one of the last sailing ships on the Great Lakes, the *Our Son,* encountered hurricane winds on Lake Michigan. With ripped sails, no radio, and a heavy load of pulpwood, she began to sink.

Acting through a "strange, subconscious force," Captain Charles H. Mohr of the southbound steamer, *William Nelson,* inexplicably altered his course. He then spotted the *Our Son* and saved the crew.

Joseph A. Sadony, a local visionary, was standing on shore miles away and is said to have directed the rescue ship to the sinking vessel through mental telepathy.

—The Bluffton Historical Society

Only he, standing on that high dune with them,
sees it. They are all holding onto their caps,
their shirts puffed out like sails, ties
lifted from their chests, trousers snapping like flags.
Only the others joke that the squall line
resembles a twisted finger thundering eastward,
only they comment on the sudden height of the waves,
whitecaps to the horizon, the biting sand.
Only they remark that no one would want
to be caught out in this storm.

He stands slightly apart, back rigid
as the mast of a schooner. The others diminish, blur,
drift away. Only this small man remains, watching
the lake turn gray, swallowed by rain. Only he
sees the ship foundering, sees the crew
holding rail, rigging, lines in terror-grip
as they wait for the sharp crack to split the beam.
Only the man at the wheel hears the directions, hears
the boat being sent to lift them from water. Only he
hears the voice calling, "Sailors, come back."

 Inland

All of us forever seeking again this warmth and this
darkness, this being alive without pain, this being alive
without anxiety or fear or aloneness.

—Anais Nin

IN FIRE

1

They are burning the tree
in the vacant lot. Flames
circle its legs, lick at dry leaves
until they bend, powder to ashes.
The tree's roots
run deep; a martyr,
its branches reach out. In the field
the only sound is crackling fire.

2

Saint Joan tied to the stake,
all white. Lilies
stretch over the field
like her virgin banner blazing in the sun.
But the punishment is for listening
to voices. The greatest vision
comes in that last echo
of unbearable heat.

3

The old crazy woman, hidden away
in the house next door.
Her face wavers
against windows as, wild-eyed,
she twists her mouth to tell children
visions. Witch, we hear her
scream through the heat of summer nights
and shut our eyes, smiling.

4

All gone, all gone. Fire
consumes us as we spread out
our arms, let flesh curl from the bones.
But roots burn slowly
and we see white visions in the flame.
Crumbling, bending to the pain, we
open our mouths, speak finally,
never know if our voice is heard.

THE LAKE ROAD

We drive along the lake road
toward water, the sky
so blue the two will blend together
at the horizon. We may never know
whether we swim or fly.

The talk is of breaking
through heat into waves, crashing
against foam. Father mother children, we will
flutter, stroke, spread out our arms,
float in again to shore.

We did not intend the splash of orange
at the road's edge, a family
of orioles scattered on the grass, broken
when they lifted, fell
in and out of currents.

The sun breaks its wings
against our windshield. On fire, we soar
over the rise to the lake.

THE END OF SUMMER

1

The old bitch labrador swims
in heavy circles. Under water
her legs run free without their limp.
She stretches brown eyes toward me,
snorting, and the stick I throw
stirs gray memories of ten Octobers,
ducks that fly at the sun and fall.

2

On the Pere Marquette River, salmon
quiver upstream from the lake, return
to alpha. At the dam
they leap and throw themselves
through currents, stretch
and spend themselves
against the torrent from the falls.

3

All week the sky has filled
with orange petals. Butterflies
floating in cycles toward milkweed,
monarchs freed from their chrysalis,
waiting for the wind's current
to die. The beach
is covered with torn wings.

4

Fire, off the merganser's hood.
This summer he nested
in our channel, drifted
with the half-tame mallards. His sharp bill
stabs water to catch bread I throw.
But he belongs by the sea. I want him
to fly now, before October and guns.

BOUNDARIES

The call of the old cock pheasant
breaks into morning. He struts the line
that marks my land from his
and I stand my ground. With hooded eyes
we dare each other to cross over.

When we beat our wings against years
a harsh cry rises in the throat. I hear
him again. He wants the brown hen.

LAST RITES

1. The Nest

We are hummingbirds and these rooms
our nest, made
of plant down and spiderwebs.
We dart back and forth to this hidden
cup of a place,
beat our tiny wings over the moment,
touch each other's ruby throats.

2. Gathering

Ritual, this day spent
at the woodcutter's, circling
his pond, throwing sticks for ecstatic dogs.
The trees are thick here, the land
still patched with spring snow.

We have eaten a country lunch:
cheese and bread, a little wine.
I find sun under some oaks
and barely hear when you kick leaves
back to the house, to old friendships
retold on the sagging couch.

But I dream of you
sorting through logs, gathering them
until, arms full, you stand before me
saying, "It's late. Time to go."
I know, without opening
my eyes, your shadow has fallen on me.

3. The Zoo

We come together
in this constriction
of cages, fences.
These moats, a protection
against saying it. Yet death
paces with the neurotic cheetah,
the buffalo's hide is scarred with it.
The snake has left its skin
and even the solarium
mutters earth in our nostrils.
Still, we pretend
until we reach the pair of lions
penned into six feet by ten,
no room to run.
Close to the bars, their eyes
hold us in narrow light.

4. Possessions

Everything sold. Oak and pine.
Plants that hung from your ceiling
and overshadowed
the woven leaves on your rug.
The iron stove that never worked.
Your desk,
jammed with letters, notes
to yourself, photos.
Gone.
Everything sold but this bed
and that promised
to the Indian woman on Friday.

IN MOURNING

This December morning is hushed.
The sky's mouth
gapes open, gray tongue
exposed, our conversation
turns brittle as milkpods. It is time
for the black dress and veils.

Last winter, our eyes
meeting could have melted icebergs.
I heard an avalanche
thunder under my skin and was terrified
of blossoming too quickly.

In March in the first thaw
I whispered my dream of you
carrying a wall, only your hands and feet
showing. Even then we recognized the signs
and touched sadly what was left.

Now this blizzard. It struck
last night while we slept.
In my garden the chrysanthemum petals
have clotted, snow hangs
from the roof of the shed. The assassin
left only one set of tracks.

THE BACK ROADS

Sunday, a crossing back
over back roads.
Slush sputters off wheels
like a covey of partridge
and our car swerves, catches
the ruts again.

All day, the blackbird
high in a winter tree,
his eye raking the snowfield.
Now, the sun gone, branches
lean, fade like smoke.
Ahead, cat eyes
burning off tree trunks.

Sometimes we see clearest
in darkness. Tonight
this wish to stay
with wild things, to follow
these twisted roads,
never cross over to Monday.

TRACING ANCESTRY AT SANDY HOOK

for Theresa

You showed an old photograph
of your grandfather, the Indian Chief,
a picture of his beaded leather vest,
his decorated wristlets, his tom-tom sticks
that your aunt keeps locked in the china cabinet.
You read from a yellowed newspaper clipping
where he said that Cherokees were artisans
and that's how he got his talent for carpentry.

You were becoming a poet that summer
and falling in love with a young black man
from New Jersey who seldom smiled.
I watched your hands meet
under the table and how you moved across the field
with him, the two of you
leaning toward each other like pine trees in a storm.
I noticed that a gull hung close to the cottage
when you sat on the porch together.

The old man. Do you think
that when he put on the ceremonial clothes
he dreamed he was capable of flight?

HEADING BACK

I move south in the thaw of land, plow a furrow
across this country. The soil turns:
Indiana loam to Georgia red clay to yellow beach again.

It is a long drive toward seas.
I need them, those gnarled trees, want to cling
to their limbs, leaf out, flower again in their shade.

"Florida sand is arid," you complain,
and your voices wither as you bend
and ache and move slowly in the garden where you live.

Each spring it is the same. I know
you no longer bear fruit,
but roots run deep, tangled under the ground.

WOUNDS

Daughters of Jerusalem, do not weep for me,
but weep for yourselves, and for your children.
                                    —Luke, ch. 23

She has been bleeding
for ten days in Mexico.
Ashamed to speak of it, she follows
the coastline with him
and covers her wound,
stops it up
like a crack in a seawall.

Smiling, touching his hand, she
pretends there is no sickness
in her belly, in that ocean
where I swam. She walks
the shore with him,
drives through dusty towns
and climbs cathedral steps.

She prays to the child and weeps
for nails in hands and feet.
Today in the kitchen, "Oh Christ,"
I cut my finger. I bound it
to stop the bleeding
and told my daughter
it was nothing.

In my sleep I am crying. Nightmares
cannot be stopped up.
There is a child
in a boat. The boat
is sinking, slipping
into the water. There is no one
to hear. The water is red.

32

SURGEONS

Those doctors are clever
with their scalpels, their nicking
their slashing.
They cut into skin
with quick knives and blood
beads like a necklace on the table.

They stitch and they tuck, tailors
in hidden rooms of the shop,
craftsmen who sew
invisible seams. Twice they have
made suits out of me,
not in the latest fashion.

Still, they have saved me
some trouble. Now
when I open the scissors
and search through wavering mirrors,
I find only a gray heap,
this bundle of worsted.

THE HOUSE THAT IS
DESERTED BY MOTHERS

Only children live here. They fold in
their long limbs and crouch, hollow-eyed,
behind doors. Hear them whimper.
They want to suckle again,
lay their heads against warm fur.
A ripening weaves in and out
of these walls like August winds,
the children turn old as withered apples.

Still, this house holds a mother's scent.
It recalls spring rain or lilacs.
You can smell it in corners. Sometimes at night
a shadow prowls among crusts of bread,
paws through stacks of laundry.
Yellow eyes bend under beds, into closets.
She is calling for babies. Listen.
She purrs now as she pads up the attic steps.

GRAND VALLEY

I have slept there with long
extended metaphors, caressed the body of syntax,
kissed simile's ear. Appetites
move with a rhythm like tides. They are
seldom satisfied. We eat, knowing we will be hungry again.

The valley fills the cup of the hand
with its gorges and meadows, its reservoirs
named after lakes. Fish swim there
almost free, tethered by invisible silver cords. They roll
in the river, fold their gills back with the current.

I have traveled to other cities
to fondle their books, proposition their young verbs.
But desire dies for weak nouns, for prepositions
that fall limp into voids. We learn
to beware of guards who station themselves near the walls.

It is back to that valley we trudge
when we feel ourselves thinning. Only there
can we dance in the fire, chew raw meat,
distill water from Indian lakes. There, baying at the moon,
we can suck eyes from all the little fish heads.

DRIVING EAST

Floating long hours over the surface
of things, the mind
drifts to fields and branches beyond.
Our car noses over bridges, past
nests of houses, cattle planted at the fence.
Shuddering against head winds
we almost forget
how it was to walk on land.

When the wind rushes by
in a thunder of feathers, I am struck
suddenly, that we are frail as birds.
Wings snapping
as they brush against trees,
breast crushed on pavement,
the soft fontanel pierced by a stone.

If the oncoming car should veer,
if he should press his foot hard
onto the pedal, if I
should permit my hands to lift off the wheel,
all motion would cease.
Your face broken
against the window, our bones
bent in strange positions of flight.

FINDING ROOTS

She is a weak sister, that ocean.
I have wasted my life
searching for kin, looking for blood
along slashes of highway. Roots

should spring from the land, I thought,
and so dug, but always reached oceans.
Scavenged the beaches, sifted
through spindrift on saltwater shores,

put shells to my ear, heard
echoes, but never my name,
found bones of coral, fossils
that bore no family ties.

And so finished by turning
inland, ebbed back to the source
away from salt, from parents
of waves that lick hardest at wounds,

North, where plants hold hard to the soil,
where ice melts slowly from glaciers.

PROWLING THE RIDGE

You, husband, lying next to
me in our bed, growl
like a wild dog or wolf
as you travel the woods
of your dream.
I feel your legs running
from or after some

thing. Now you turn
and curl toward the moon.
Away from me, you
prowl along ridges, hunt
with the pack. You rest
your paws on wild fur, bare
teeth to raw meat.

If I reach out and touch
the curve of your haunch,
brush my hand over your skin,
I can tame you
back to this room, to this wife
still outside
your blanket of sleep.

But it's your dream
I burn for, the other
place and time.
Wolf, leave tracks now. Quick.
Let me follow your scent.

CONJOINED

a marriage poem

The onion in my cupboard, a monster, actually
two joined under one transparent skin:
each half-round, then flat and deformed
where it pressed and grew against the other.

An accident, like the two-headed calf rooted
in one body, fighting to suck at its mother's teats;
or like those other freaks, Chang and Eng, twins
joined at the chest by skin and muscle, doomed
to live, even make love, together for sixty years.

Do you feel the skin that binds us
together as we move, heavy in this house?
To sever the muscle could free one,
but might kill the other. Ah, but men
don't slice onions in the kitchen, seldom see
what is invisible. We cannot escape each other.

ICE STORM

The second day, we don't even
look up when light strikes
west of us and winter thunder erupts.
How quickly we crawl inside in this weather.

At first, the trees accept their new skins.
But by the third day, they can't
bear the weight. They begin
to bend, bow down to the sleet, and we

hunch like stones over the breakfast table.
The first to go is the birch, one branch
on the road, another on the driveway.
Then the silver maple falls apart.

But when the willow splits in threes
like an overripe tulip, only its two-foot stump
still stuck in the frozen earth,
we break out and run, keening, to touch the wound.

Later, when the sun finally shows its face,
we gather limbs and find
the few faint buds that had exposed themselves.

FOR JOSEPH, WHO WROTE
A POEM ABOUT WILD STRAWBERRIES

This morning, wild raspberries for breakfast
picked by my daughter and her friend.
One girl is blond, the other brunet, each
small-breasted, with hips beginning to round.

While I was still uncurling, they bent
at the edge of the woods
and pulled tiny buds from their stems.
A whole pan of them.
Each berry released, suddenly become a cup
and their lips stained, their mouths
puckered from the sweet,
from the sour of the juice.

A month ago, one evening at the beach,
an empty stretch on Lake Michigan,
these girls flung their clothes on the sand
and dropped shyly into waves.
The lake was rough, tossed them
back again. And they, not yet tame,
screamed and fought, then coyly limp,
let the water take them.

As they ran toward me at sunset, I saw
how ripe they were, their skin patched by tans
made in bathing suits, the dark
shadows where their legs sprouted,
the tiny buds of their breasts. And I was ashamed
of my own body, still wrapped in cloth.

You, Joseph, write about wild strawberries becoming art
and that, I suppose, is a part of this poem too.
After breakfast today we walked to the edge
of the woods, my daughter, her friend,
and I: three women who know about gathering.

The bushes were so plain,
thorny, and clogged with spiderwebs,
the veined leaves not even spectacular.
In a few days the raspberries will be gone
and the plants will look like scrub
to anyone who doesn't know.
But this morning I poured milk
over the berries, watched it purple
in the bottom of my bowl.

DAGUERREOTYPE

November, and this country road
still brown, the reflection
pearling in puddles.

Cornfields like an old man's beard,
Queen Anne's lace tattered and stained,
a slow muting
when the chestnut horse
sags in front of the raw house.

It is as if
all color had been drained
from the eye. Beyond the field

nests are exposed
and a muffled explosion ruffles the trees.
Brown bodies rise up,
float, and branches
of antlers settle on fallen leaves.

But the heart
flutters like a sparrow's wing.

# Yellow Dog

Not for naught the dog is barking,
Never has he barked for nothing,
Never growls he at the fir-trees.
—Runo XVIII, *Kalevala*

YELLOW DOG: THE RIVER

I

When Barry found the dog
on his roof, he took it
as a sign, fed it steak and strawberries.
Hearing him tell it that day, I knew
I would go, that the dog
came for me as well.

Nine hours by car, but always
toward water, a pulling back
to streams of copper and pine.
The river runs north
and high in the spring. It spills
trout at every bend.

Sirius warms the winter sky, two dogs
who follow the hunter through snowy nights.
It was February and the dog
was shivering. He did not
come again. We never knew
how he climbed the roof.

Even in the south he is
a sign: "Where the Southern
cross the Yellow Dog." A code
in blues, special language for blacks.
To be inside the symbol
was to live on tracks that ran north.

The land was meant
to be lumbered, three climax forests.
My father and his brother built the camp,
no electricity or running water.
Each summer the man left Detroit
and, homing, drove back to his place.

Look at the medieval tombs
of married women. If the wife died faithful,
a dog was carved at her feet.
So we are marked,
even in death, his absence
like a scar across the cheek.

II

One morning to cross the palm:
Fate line through Saturn, then out
over water. Floating
the bridge, breath suspended over narrows.
When the sun begins its fall,
the hand closes behind me.

I am daughter
of Nordic fathers, aging mother
who creeps back to her land. Deep,
deeper in woods, the river
blazes yellow and runs hard.
A howl raises in my throat.

Yellow Dog out of Bull Dog
Lake, a bastardization
of something like *jaune chien*.
Fed by the Big and Little Pups, its skin
stirs with French, Indians, Finns:
shadows of priests, loggers, trappers.

Tin Can Sullivan. Billy Bushey,
the seventeen-year-old counterfeiter.
Baraga, the Snowshoe Priest.
10 O'Clock Charlie. Good-Looking Tom.
They knew the river's gold. It shines
twenty-four carat in the noon sun.

Twice burned out, first
White Pine, then Jack, now Maple.
Tin Can blew his head off in '28.
Billy had a trap door
in his cabin, dipped water
from the creek summer and winter.

49

Below the seven falls, down
from Bushey Creek, the dog bares his teeth
over ore. I cast out
at the bend,
watch the fly float downstream,
and growl as water runs cold at my heels.

III

All night, wild things
circled the cabin. In sleep
I saw a wolf's orange eyes, heard an owl moan.
This morning I find arrow prints
of deer, black droppings of mice,
the bear's scent outside my door.

Not yet grandmother,
still in tattered rags of child,
I rock in my blanket and listen
to the dog run past my clearing.
Wind hangs in the woods,
the whitethroat calls.

For a week I followed the riverbank
through the canyon of the falls,
over brown pine needles and hard,
sharp, jagged rocks.
I dug my heels into the fur of his sand,
washed in his biting water.

Tomorrow, a crossing back
into the palm, to those deep lines
that tie. Women are bound to cycles,
yet a power rises
in the moon's reflection on water,
when water flows over ore.

Even when I nursed my young,
I followed the steps of the old ones.
The path always led here. This river,
born barking on the plains,
ends with Superior
waiting to fold it in waves,
to gather its Yellow Dog home again.

BLACK BEAR

Bears make love to women alone by the sea.
—Robert Bly

Looming up from old dreams, a hundred
black shapes
of honey lovers, of clumsy dancers
in coats that ripple too large,
of peanut beggars who lift paws behind zoo fences.

More than a dozen times he has
roamed the corners of my yard, reared up, charged.
Sometimes I save children, often myself,
but always I wake
with sweat warm on my palms, fear rising off the bed.

Alone in the woods.
Copper country, my shoes turn rusty after an hour.
A wrong path. I go deeper,
but never reach the lake, though it rises
twice through trees and I smell the waves.

Coming out, a branch cracks. His black head
sinks in the brush. Fur lifts on my neck
and I stir, waking. A stick, three stones, my knife.
I stammer upwind past the burned-out tree stumps,
past his prints in the mud.

Long winters he sleeps. This spring
I stand at the edge and wait.
He growls. I step closer. A shadow rears up.
So we face each other, our breath heaving.
It is never easy.

RAVEN

He has set his seal upon my face.
—*Posuit Signum*

I

For three days his shrieks
ripped through the woods. And I,
not knowing what or who, would miss a step
in the cabin, still my cup
between table and lips, hold breath near the ribs.

Things turn when you're alone.
Smoke doesn't rise, trees walk at night.
Sometimes the mind twists into grotesque shapes.

On Thursday then, in a gash
above the falls, his shadow crossed the river
and he opened his throat to me.
I held myself in his dark circle,
was caught by the thrust of his beak.

II

Child in veil and white dress, a taking in.
The wafer melts on my tongue.
Later, other sacraments.
Words spill from my mouth, but they twist,
grow ragged, scatter like feathers.

Now that he has found where I live, he will always
be here. I creep under his wings
and he follows, ruffling robes, reciting matins.

If I open the door, he will perhaps
swoop down and enter, this box
of a house the place of annointment.
Kneeling, lips to the river's curtain,
I begin the ablution, the crossing over.

BEFORE COMPLETION

She pretends there is no fur
bristling off the belly, no
elongation of her jaw when the wind bites,
no tiny glitter inside her eye.
Yet she stands under the frigid moon,
sends growls across the lake.
   She paces the edge:
   Fire on snow,
   fire on water.
Gray fox waiting for the lake to freeze,
miles across thin ice to the other shore.
When she howls at your door
open it, pour red wine for warmth,
kiss the cut pads of her feet.

WINTER POEM/THE SNOWY OWL

1. The Dream/The Need

White on white, it feathers
in layers,
silk folding over silk.
No detail, but the sense
of snow
exploding out of snow.

The sleeper floats within
the dream. White sound
soars from the gaping "O"
of the mouth, all motion
held beyond the outstretched arm
that rises, the cry
sinking into the pillow,
the sheet fluttering,
a cloud against bones.

Blink of yellow light, breath
suspended.
Wings falter, it falls.
The eye
opens, the head revolves,
stares dumbly into winter.

2. The Cold/The Motion

This will be their hardest season.
Wind slants, beats snow in circles,
heaves drifts against the house.
She whimpers, but holds the weight and bears
witness to trees bending, to a lake
that sinks into armor. What was
descends. The surface freezes.

She spins inward in the lamplight,
spreads hands over the flame, and speaks
of flight, of something like a cloud
floating over the tundra. Her eyes slit,
round. She tells him she loves him,
though she no longer believes in words.
Tiny animals skitter, become what is hunted.

3. The Hunt/The Pattern

Waiting is the backbone of winter.
Pale light from sun and moon. Cold
whips at skirts, the entrance to sleeves
Days whirl by without shadow.
She leans into the lash, it coils around her.

Flutter of white by the river. She reels
through drifts like a derelict.
Not him, only snow on a log.
Here, dark things define themselves:
bridge, bare willows lacing the bank,
stump locked in ice near lowland.

It was a mistake to speak of poems
and white owls in a breath, foolish
to count on patterns for a cure, on feathers
that might be gathered off the snow,
ghosts of words waiting to be written.
She returns without him.

4. The Light/The Presence

He comes when she least expects him,
like a lover, out of night into morning.
When he flies by her window she thinks she hears thunder
and claps her hands to her face. She does not see
his shadow melt into the snow.

He waits in the corner of her garden.
She trembles on the threshold, unable
to go there, to step inside his wings.

White on white, feathers like silk,
the head turns slowly. In winter
dreams hide beneath blankets, only the eyelids glow
yellow chrysanthemums. At last she sees
how fire burns from within and steps forward.
His eyes ignite, the flame rises.

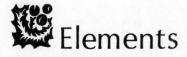# Elements

The old man tunes his drum between the bowl of fire and the bowl of water, listening to the music that is about to come.

—Robert Duncan

HEIGHTS

O human race, born to fly upward,
wherefore at a little wind dost
thou so fall?
　　　　　　　　　—Dante

1

Falling, hanging by my feet
upside down
from the basement stairs.
My mother at the ironing board,
her back turned,
the cry for help
falling from my mouth.
So close
I could almost touch her,
she would not turn.

2

My friend flew
in the minister's bed, a bird
drifting over ice floes.
He woke when he urinated,
ten years old, ashamed.

3

When he was a boy
in Muskegon, my husband
climbed Pigeon Hill and jumped,
hovered
before sand thudded up, the grains
fuzzing like down on his skin.
That dune is flat now, hauled away
by the boatload and sold.

4

Another time I stood
at the top of the stairs,
arms spread out,
and stepped off.
Flying is floating,
I did
to the bottom.
No one saw. I never
could do it again.

5

At Mont Blanc, steps
carved out of ice. Snow
fell all day up there.
We hung skis over our shoulders and clung
to the rope as we climbed,
held ourselves
from looking down the crevasse.

6

We grow afraid
to speak of it,
forget that we wore capes
once, and leaped
from swings in the backyard.
We close our fists
and fall away.

7

When the Wallenda pyramid broke,
the family
floated in feathers
to the circus floor.
Karl, the old man, still walks
the cable, sometimes between hotels in Florida.
We tilt our heads back to study the tiny steps,
we whisper
perverse words of flight.

BURNING AGAINST THE WIND

You must burn against the wind, always, and burn slowly.
—Henry David Thoreau

1

In this falling of seasons,
I hunch against the wind toward forty.

2

Since morning
the brown squirrel, dead
on the road,
tail lifting
in the draft of cars, innards
singing from his mouth.

3

At the lake, gulls
turn their backs
to the sunset, feathers
set against gale winds.

4

Ships go down
in October, the beginning
of storms from the north.
They cast off, the proud bows head west
and run before broken seas.

5

A blanket
breaks over my lawn.
Slow falling, this sewing of patches
on my green bed.

6

Sailors
call for mother
as waves fold over them.

7

Fox fire glows on the hill
out of old wood, long seasons.

8

Leaves curl in
toward the flame, eyes
of tiny animals,
children's voices crying in the night.

9

If I open my coat, will you
kiss my breasts warm,
help me lean against this wind?

REQUIEMS

1

The flower opens
its petals, one by one:
purple, lavender, then pink,
until the black stamen is exposed.

2

They will not rest,
those mothers,
they call for their blood.
I bow my head,
cross myself in the thicket,
and beg them to sleep.

3

Wolf, follow their scent,
crouch low
to the ground, howl
for the place that was theirs.

4

Groping for water.
Wild things suffer
from thirst. Drink
and the river runs
red in the mouth.

5

Shuffle the dusty path,
grave to tired house.
Carry water from the spring,
carry infants over the threshold.

6

Bees
heavy with pollen,
field to garden.
The queen lays her eggs. Honey forms
in cells of the hive.

7

Inside, I listen at doors,
test floorboards with feet,
lie down on the marriage bed, open
arms to wailing children.

8

A smell of bread
lifts from the stove like murmuring voices.
Rest in peace, old ones.

9

Outside, scurrying
in bushes, the moon
crumbles behind ashes.
A sighing
encircles me
and I am no longer certain
about tree roots and branches. Bones
go soft, then brittle.

10

Pace from mound to house
again, the light in the window,
their rooms. The power rises.

11

Seeds fall from the flower.
Corn is harvested.
Plants fold into themselves,
spring forth in other seasons.

12

I will live in my daughter. The woman
burns like a fetus within the girl.
She bends with the weight. She begins
to feel me, that one,
as she hoods her eyes against the flame
and her mouth grows fierce.

13

The boy moves with a warrior's grace.
Already, he speaks in tongues
and a sharp light burns behind his eyes.
Words I have known
fall like petals from his lips.

14

The final turning is to
moss and dry leaves,
the breath of rotting wood,
a tending.

IN THE PRESENCE OF MOTHERS

1

Squall lines, laboring,
roll one on the other
out from the island.
Nightmares
out of depths and old drownings,
they rise
with crooning winds,
watery arms.
The breasts of them
weigh against our bones.

2

Cradled
at the shore's arm,
we fold into the sweet
breath of her hum
and dream
through flashes of light. Her fury
rocks us.

3

Madonna of the stable,
open the sky to a star
so that we may kneel in the confession box
and cross ourselves with prism points.
Infants become saviors
in their first taste of milk.

4

In the harbor's barn
our sea-mare
shudders in her stall, flanks
quivering, mast to belly.
Again, *la mer*
calls this horse.
Obedient child, break loose
your reins, ride high over waves, rise
in the trail of her hair.

5

Black into light and back,
the sun rises and falls in its tedium.
But the delicate stars,
they nurse us
along the moon's yellow path
into hard arms, new openings.

6

Lovely seasons.
After rain, snow
sails down in tiny boats.
Silence of cold, a falling
of tears. Still
arms lift out of ice:
the sorrow of it,
the loss.

7

Back and back, past all
hard rocks and caves, down
into the loam of her skin.
She stirs under the sea
and we enter the way we came,
crying, through cold
to the inner place,
the long warmth of the woman.

PITT POETRY SERIES

Ed Ochester, General Editor